DITCH THE SCRUBS

Presents

SUCCESS
SECRETS

To Running a $10 Million Home Care Agency

CHRISTINE BACCI

Cover design by Ivica Jandrijevic
Interior layout and design by Clark Kenyon

ISBN: 978-1-7373323-3-6 (Paperback)
978-1-7373323-4-3 (eBook)

Published by Ditch the Scrubs Press

Although the author and publisher have made every effort to ensure that
the information in this book was correct at press time, neither author
nor publisher assumes any liability to any party for any loss, damage,
or disruption caused by errors or omissions, whether such errors or
omissions result from negligence, accident, or any other cause. Both
author and publisher hereby disclaim any liability to any party. Readers
should contact their attorney to obtain advice before pursuing any
course of action.

Contents

Foreword

Having been in healthcare for more than 20 years of my life, I feel like I have done a lot- from Long Term Care to hospitals, ventilator babies, wound care, acute care, education, and end of life care. I have been an entrepreneur for even longer – from the time I was 12 and walked the neighborhood selling magazines and gift-wrap to when I was 18 and opened my first restaurant. Entrepreneurship is in my blood. There is no where I go, even on vacation, that my mind is not analyzing the situation and possibilities and thinking of how much money the business generates and whether or not its something I want to do. It has been both a blessing and a curse! I would have to live three lifetimes to do all that I want to do!

But when I look back over the last 21+ years of this journey, one thing is certain. I wish I could talk to that young girl who was determined but so clueless. I wish that I could give her even one single pearl of wisdom for her journey. That pearl that I would have given her and that I will share with you now is this – Find Knowledge and Wisdom at all times and at all costs! This book is a compilation of wisdom and knowledge that I gained along the journey. Wisdom that I wished I had known to look for 20 years ago! There is not a goal you can undertake in your life that someone has not gone before you and been there and done that. Why should you have to figure everything out along the way – when someone has already gone before you? Do you understand that by purposefully staying in pursuit of knowledge, you can avoid costly mistakes – both with your time, effort, and money?

I have learned that Pride and ignorance stand in the way of us asking for help and knowledge. Pride because we think we already know what we are doing and ignorance because you can't possibly know What You Do Not Know. If I had learned the skill of always purposefully seeking knowledge and wisdom from any source before each of my ventures, I would have been a millionaire long before I turned 40. This book is my gift to you of some of the hard-earned lessons I have learned over the years.

Although I have successfully ran a Homecare agency for more than 15 years, in 2018, after closing our restaurant ventures, I began again. After finishing 2017 with only $200,000 in Homecare revenue, I applied a focused effort and in 2018 we had grown to $2.2 Million. In 2019, we more than doubled and increased to $5.5 Million and in 2020, the year of the pandemic, despite every obstacle that you can imagine and probably relate to, we finished the year at $8 Million dollars. As of May 2021, the time of the writing of this book, we have already hit $5 Million in revenue and will soar past $10 Million this year. I don't say this to brag. I want you to understand the growth that is absolutely possible to not only me but you! We grew from $200,000 in annual revenue to more than $10 Million in just over 3 years by applying the principles in this book. These lessons are my secret sauce and exactly what we had to evaluate and apply, over and over, to achieve this level of growth.

However, be warned! The very first chapter in this book asks you to evaluate how much is enough for YOU. There is no ruler that everyone has to stand next to be measured for success. The size of your agency has to match your lifestyle goals. I am a Capricorn that thinks, lives, and breaths work – it literally never stops going in my mind, much to my husband's chagrin! So, just because something has worked for me does not mean that it has to work for you. Sift through the pearls I offer and find what speaks to you. Mine through the rubble and find the treasure buried within. Don't make the mistake of ignoring a section or chapter because you think it doesn't apply or because you think you already know something. I can't tell you how many times I have had an A-ha moment over a wisdom pearl that I already knew or had heard before! Sometimes it takes being at a different place in our mindset to be able to really absorb something that we heard before.

All it takes is one moment in time, one word, one A-Ha, and everything can change. Open the ears of your heart and mind and purposefully pursue Wisdom and Knowledge. I wish you every good thing and all success in your journey as a Homecare Agency owner!

Christine Bacci

CHAPTER 1

Bigger is not Better

Too many times, Homecare Agency owners think that they have to continuously work to gain more clients. If I could only get another 1,000 billable hours becomes a goal without an end in sight. When there is poor financial planning, and expenses that exceed the agency's revenue or the owner's lifestyle creep, the NEED to continually work to increase your agency's revenue can never end. Or you hear about another agency that did $2 Million or $5 Million in annual revenue and get a case of FOMO that sends you back on the hustle to grow and find more clients. But I have news for you – Bigger is not always Better!

I will never be the consultant who tells you that the sky is not the limit. I work to encourage and push entrepreneurs and those around me past their comfort zone all the time. I think that we constantly need to ask ourselves have we given our all and done our best. However, owning and running a Homecare agency, while rewarding, can be extremely demanding. I will be honest with you – managing a Homecare agency can feel like the ultimate test of patience and skill. You will have days that you are on top of the world and the very next day come crashing down to realize that all the hard work you put into earning the trust of a client was undermined by one caregiver, costing you thousands of dollars in revenue. I count tell you how many times I have heard agency owners say that they feel like just closing the doors or selling their dream, just to be free. For as much as I want to encourage you to push yourself beyond what you think you are capable of, I also want to teach you to find the sweet spot for you.

Being an entrepreneur is great, but from the start you must have some clearly defined goals. What does financial freedom look like to you? How much money do you need to make each month to be able to not only be comfortable, but also enjoy it? After all, it does you no good to tell the world that you have made $100,000 last month when you had to work 18-hour days for 29 days in a row. What good is money that you can't enjoy? Ask yourself the tough questions – How much is too much? How much do you need to survive? How much to have more freedom than what you have now – the freedom to take a day or a week off just because you want to; the freedom to book a flight to Vegas for 4 days – just because you heard there was a new restaurant opening; or the freedom to take off and help watch grandchildren for a week. What financial goal do you need to set that allows you to make enough money to live, save, splurge and still be able to leave the office every day by 4pm?

I want to challenge your thinking on growth – It's easy to think that your business' growth is THE measure of success. But, I want to tell you that sometimes growth can actually be your enemy and ultimately cause to become unsuccessful at what matters most – building your business and source of income around your life and happiness. Here are 5 reasons why you might consider limiting your Homecare Agency's growth:

1. **Growth can create unnecessary complex obstacles and cycles**
   A Homecare Agency that is small is controllable. The more clients you serve, the more caregivers you will need to hire. The more caregivers you need to hire – in today's time of dire shortage – the more hassle and headache you will have to find what has become unicorns in a sea of employable people. The more caregivers and clients you have in common, the more people you will need in your inner circle

of administrative support to manage them. The greater burden on your overhead and the more clients you will need to add to increase revenue enough to sustain your profits causes the whole process to repeat itself. Do you see the cycle? It quickly becomes never-ending.

2. **Smaller can often times last longer**
Your company's ability to weather the continuously changing climate of healthcare can be affected by its size. The larger you are and particularly if that growth was quickly gained, can leave your agency with cracks in its foundation and operating systems that can show signs of wear and tear and began to crumble from the strain placed on them. Smaller agencies are at an advantage of being able to pivot and make crucial necessary changes that ultimately can increase their sustainability and longevity. One of example of this was my $10 million dollar agency with 300 clients and 400 employees. At one point, we were gaining clients so quickly that we were unable to offer our signature detailed service. We were matching caregivers and clients and allowing them to set their own schedules that we had no knowledge of. Can you guess what happened? As our number of billable hours grew, the number of hours actually billed began to drop. It didn't make sense and took us almost 6 months to realize that the change in our system's procedure had undermined our structure. We were allowing our finances to be dependent on undependable new people. Despite the rapid growth, had we slowed down acceptance of new clients long enough to allow our systems to be maintained, we would have avoided months of chaos, and had we not recognized the problem at all, we would have quickly lost enough money to threaten our company's stability.

3. **You can be selective on what clients and caregivers to accept**
When you have purposely chosen to remain small, you retain the freedom and flexibility of being able to choose which clients to accept.

You can choose a specific niche and become the premier provider of that group in your area, developing your expertise. Being the specialist for a particular group will only make you more desired. You can be selective on the caregivers you accept and the standards you maintain when you have a smaller group to oversee.

4. **You are able to grow your revenue without having to grow your overhead**

It is a fact – the more clients and caregivers you have, the higher your overhead costs will be. You will need more support staff for staffing, billing, nursing, HR, etc… The more staff you have the more trappings you have to offer that ultimately cost the agency – medical insurance benefits, paid time off, vacation time, and bonuses. All of these quickly add up and begin to subtract from your bottom line. A company with 50 or fewer employees can offer benefits they choose to offer that make financial sense for them rather than be required to offer them.

5. **You can spend more time with friends and family**

Face it. Close to the top of your list for wanting to start your own Homecare agency is the desire for freedom. The desire to control your lifestyle and choices and to be able to have more time with your family. By controlling your growth, you will be able to maintain the growth over your lifestyle that a larger company focused on growth simply cannot. You must create your own definition of success and then mold your business to fit your design rather than letting the business grow uncontrollably and you having to change your lifestyle to meets its changing demands.

Remember, you started this journey to gain freedom, not to chain yourself to another job with a fancy label. I challenge you to think long and hard about what defines your goals – If you previously made

$55,000 a year as a Registered Nurse and you are able to increase that to $250,000 by owning a Homecare Agency (which would be an agency that generates around $1-1.2M annually) – why is that not enough? You just increased your annual income by 5X!! Truthfully look at your budget and spending and see if you have allowed lifestyle creep to happen in your life.

Lifestyle Creep

Lifestyle creep is something that can sneak up on you if you are not aware of what it is and remain vigilant to watch for its warning signs. When you hit your first month of earning a $10,000 plus profit, it is so easy to think that you need to celebrate. You tell yourself that you deserve to splurge after all the sacrifices that you have made to get this far. It's perfectly normal to want to buy new clothes, a new car or house, and to eat out more. You rationalize that you "need" a housekeeper, or a nanny, and prepackaged meals. While it's perfectly okay to reward yourself for your hard work and to enjoy life hacks like help with housework, it's also important to keep an eye on the bigger financial freedom picture.

Lifestyle creep, also known as lifestyle inflation, can sneak up on you and prevent you from ever truly finding financial freedom. Instead, it can be so sneaky that the only reward you will find you have earned is a pair of handcuffs to your new business and the struggle to have to constantly earn more. The more money you earn, especially if you have never earned as much income before in the past, you have to learn to become vigilant at preventing it from leaving as quick as it comes in. When you have an abundance, it is easy to think that the supply will never end.

You must remember that everything comes with a cost. Let's look at the costs to have your million dollar dream home (California and NY I am not talking to you as I know a dream home can run $3-5 million!):

- Higher mortgage – even with 2021's historically low interest rates, a $1 million dollar home will run you around $4,500/month
- Property Tax and insurance – these costs can run you thousands of dollars per year - $2,000
- Outdoor maintenance – Weekly lawn care and pool maintenance costs can cost several hundred each month - $500/month
- Cleaning – The more thousands of square feet you have, the more likely you will have to add the expense of housekeepers - $1,400/month
- Upkeep and Repairs – Estimate anywhere from $1000-2000/month

We won't even add in the cost of new furnishings and decorations for your new home that you HAVE to have and we are already at close to $9,500/month!

The more stuff you buy, the more you have to spend to maintain it. The more stuff you buy, the more you think you just cannot live without it and non-essential items quickly come to be thought of as essential. You will convince yourself that you just cannot function throughout the day without your morning Starbucks coffee and tea that costs you $10/day. And the higher your lifestyle costs to maintain, the more indebt you will be to your business. You will find that you can't take time off and you can't enjoy the fruits of your labor because you are in a never-ending cycle of needing to earn more to support your new lifestyle costs that creeped up on you. I warn you!

How to avoid lifestyle creep:

1. **Write down your goals** – only you know what your financial goals are. Whether that be to pay for your children's college education, to purchase a new home, or going on a dream vacation – having a list

of clearly defined goals will help you to decide if an expense will help or hinder you from reaching those goals.

2. **Reward yourself responsibly.** Absolutely treat yourself to something that you have always wanted to do or purchase. Spend intentionally and always asks yourself if there will be further financial commitment required for your purchase. If you choose to purchase a foreign car, know that you will have to pay 2-3x the normal price for something as simple as an oil change. Resist impulse buying.

3. **Pay yourself first!** Ensure that you have an emergency fund of 6 months to one year's expenses, and then make additional deposits into your retirement fund. As an entrepreneur, it is critical that you don't neglect the important task of preparing for the day that you don't have to work again – a healthy retirement account balance will ensure that you will achieve this goal. Pay yourself before any large purchase or extra expense. I recommend setting this up to be an automatic contribution. By doing so, you will not even miss this money. It will help to ensure that you continue to get by on your preestablished budget.

4. **Set a pre-determined amount for YOUR budget/paycheck to live on.** Pay yourself with a pre-determined paycheck or draw. Determine your living expenses, any discretionary spending, and a fun budget and stick to it! Pay yourself this amount every week or month through a payroll deposit or draw from your company revenue. Whatever you do – stick to it! Make your lifestyle fit your budget, not the other way around.

5. **Surround yourself with people who understand and will help you be accountable.** It is so easy to think that you have "arrived" when you start to see 5 and 6 figures in your bank account at your disposal. But

by having a support system in place that can provide accountability and maintaining relationships you had prior to "arriving" will help to ensure that you make financially sound decisions. Regularly meet with your accountant to ensure that your spending and saving are in line with your financial goals.

Success as a Homecare agency is different for each of us.
Once you know your personal goals and lifestyle choices, you simply
need to know when it makes sense to grow and when it doesn't –
for you personally.

CHAPTER 2

Why Homecare Agencies Fail

Starting a Homecare agency carries risks with no guarantees which is why not all Homecare agencies are successful. According to the US Small Business Administration, only 59% of Homecare agencies started will survive their first 3 years and that number drops to 48% who will survive for 5 years. These odds can be scary if you are new to the business.

Passion, energy, and excitement that many new owners bring when they start their own agency are simply not enough to ensure success. I cannot tell you how many times I have seen people say they have a Homecare agency but they haven't done this yet, or they don't have this. Or they ask a question that is so basic in nature, I know that their agency must have serious cracks in its structural foundation. Understanding what it takes to be successful as an agency owner is crucial to your chances of not only surviving your first years in business but thriving.

There are many reasons that businesses fail to survive their first year and most are common to all industries – not just Home Care. Here are the most common reasons:

Lack of Money
The number one reason that Homecare agencies fail is because they run out of money. This is usually caused because Homecare agencies fail to recognize and plan for all the costs involved in starting an agency. The only way to

reduce the risk is to create a realistic financial plan. This includes knowing your startup costs and at what point you will reach profitability. You must know how much money you will need for living expenses and how much money you need from the time of start-up to profitability. Once you have this plan, you must stick to it!

I see a lot of people jump headfirst into the idea of starting their own Homecare agency on a wish and prayer. While there is nothing wrong with stepping out on Faith, there must be a sense of reality that balances it all. If you are the only person who supports your living expenses, it is not a good idea to quit your job to start a Homecare agency with no savings. Ideally, you will have a savings fund that you can use to support you during the most crucial time of startup. If you have family support, even better. Set your finances up so that you can live off the income of only one person, allowing you the best chance at success with your new agency.

Beware of the following:

- **Too much overhead** – when you start your agency, you won't be able to afford to hire a marketer, biller, staffer, and receptionist. You have to be prepared to be all of these things until you have your first few clients. Your revenue should dictate your overhead and your hiring of support staff. Beware of basing your overhead on growth projections! Always work to increase your revenue before adding additional overhead. Set goals – when I get 120 billable hours (which could be as few as 3 clients), I will add my first office staff member and won't add my second client until I have 400 hours. (You and one other person could easily support 400 billable hours – approximately 10 40-hour clients) By doing so, your expense is matched with increasing revenue.

- **Personal use of Business Funds** – One of the biggest mistakes you can make is intermingling your business and personal funds. From a tax perspective it is a huge disaster if you are audited by the IRS – they will eat you alive and you risk important expense deductions being lost which could ultimately increase your tax. It is a messy practice that is a hard habit to break and you risk developing a habit of living off cash flow and fooling yourself into thinking you are profitable. You also undermine your agency's financial stability by not having a budget that you are able to stick to. If you plan properly and stick to the plan, you will have a set amount that you pay yourself from the business and keep your funds SEPARATE. You must maintain separate bank accounts for your personal and business needs.

- **Over-investing** – You don't need the fancy laptop and to purchase your first office building. You can rent a small space that is affordable and fits your budget. You don't have to have a $1000 glass desk with matching Chanel decorative bookends. Your spending has to match your budget. Don't set out trying to impress others with a look you think you need to have – it could cost you your business.

Do you see the theme here? By simply failing to plan a budget that you can stick to, you are planning to fail.

Lack of a Business Plan or a Poor one

You would never expect a builder to build a house without a plan, so why would you go into business without one? I have seen the question asked by someone new, "Do I really need a business plan?" and seen people tell them no, that they paid someone to make one and never used it, and I often wish to know how that was working for them. A business plan can be a huge undervalued asset to a new Homecare agency. It doesn't matter if your agency is already running or if you are about to start one. You must have a plan that you are going to follow and it's never too late to create one. The Bible says, "My people perish for lack of knowledge," I say, your agency can fail without a plan in place.

You need a business plan that thinks about not only your ultimate goals –

How much revenue do you want to make this year, but:
Your future plans -how long you plan to run your agency;
What challenges you can expect to face- nationwide caregiver shortage in the face of the pandemic; and
How you will accomplish your goals.
Your business plan should cover details like who your local competition is, how your agency will be organized, how you will market, and how you will manage your employment issues.

Think of your business plan like a road map. You would never set out to drive 1,000 miles without a map to show you the way. Don't start or run your business without one either. Your business plan should have structure, but should also be flexible, changing over time to meet your needs and adopt new goals and strategies. Every month, quarter, and year you should have a planned guide to follow to ensure that you agency will reach its goals.

The Inability to Translate Caregiving Skills into Business Skills

Many agency owners start their business because they are natural caretakers. You may have worked in Homecare before as a CNA, HHA, LPN, or RN or have experience caring for your own loved one. But being a caregiver and a business owner are two completely different skill sets. Just because you are good at one does not mean that you are going to be good at the other. It is imperative that as an agency owner you recognize your strengths and weaknesses and hire employees to fill in the gaps. You must have people on your team with the skills that you lack – whether that be in accounting and billing, employee management, or marketing your agency. Napolean Hill tells the story of Henry Ford, who created the Ford Motor company. Henry only ever achieved an 8th grade education but had an aptitude for mechanics and vision. He realized that he did not have the knowledge required to build transmissions but believed it could be done. So, he surrounded himself with the smartest people he could find and put them to work to create what he envisioned. Be Henry Ford! Acknowledge your weaknesses and surround yourself with people who fill the gaps.

Failing to Invest in Marketing

Many agency owners think that successful marketing is simply handing out some flyers and business cards, when in reality that is far from the truth. Your conversion rate from simple flyers and business cards will actually be quite low. Failing to understand that marketing is actually about building your brand and relationships could be one reason that your agency is not growing or can ultimately fail. If you do not have the salesmanship and relationship building skills and time, you should strongly consider hiring someone to manage this important foundation of your agency's success. It's not just about developing new relationships with referral sources, but sustaining them for the long-term.

Failing to Invest in an Agency Software Management System

It doesn't matter which one you choose, but it is absolutely crucial to the success of your agency to have software system in place to help you manage your agency. I can not tell you how many years I survived managing our agency with pen and pencil. I could cry a river at just how hard I was working by lacking systems that could have easily helped to improve my efficiency and productivity. Lack of a management system could lead to you failing to be compliant with your regulations – keeping up with employee backgrounds, client supervisory visits, employee missed shifts and key billing information. One year, we estimated that we lost over $100,000 in missed billing to Medicaid by simply failing to have a system that ensured that all money billed was actually received. This is one investment that you should not avoid.

Lack of Critical Support Roles

As I mentioned earlier, failing to surround yourself who either complement your abilities or fill in the gaps can lead to an agency's lack of success. Many startup agency owners try to do it all – often due to a lack of money. They try to do all the marketing, client intakes, billing, payroll, scheduling, and often times will even work to cover shifts with clients. Surely you can see where this ends – burn out, loss of revenue, and overall chaos. You cannot do it all and you most certainly do not know it all. Don't fool yourself into believing otherwise. Later in this book, in chapter The Master of Everything, we will go over critical roles within your agency that you must ensure are filled to increase your chances for success.

Lack of Oversight/Work

I can't tell you how often I have seen a business owner take the opposite of approach of trying to do it all – doing nothing at all. They make the mistake of thinking that all they have to do is hire enough people and the work will get done. Magic, right? Unfortunately, this extreme can also lead to disaster. By being hands off too early, and even later after having established your agency if left in the wrong hands, you risk your agency's success on a team without a guide. No one will ever run your business the way that you would. They won't treat it with the same regard or approach decisions with the mindset of an owner if they are not the owner.

A Homecare agency is not something that you can open and go about your business, expecting that it can run itself. It is a business model that centers around people and constantly changing scenarios. I had a friend with an agency that had built it up into a $2 million dollar company and she decided that she wanted to sell cars and start a second business. She left her agency in the hands of her office team only to look up a year later and realize that her $2 million dollar company was only generating around $500,000. Because she had not been involved in the business much over the course of that year, even when she committed to building her agency up again, she had no idea where to start and what area of management had fallen apart. While the goal IS build a team of competent, dependable staff who can run your agency while you are away so that you are not chained to a job, you still should not expect that you can just walk away and everything will remain status quo.

Lack of Business Operating Systems

Your agency must have a Business Operation System. These are a series of defined processes that include the structure, principles, and practices that drive your agency. Systems ensure that daily work is focused on your agency's strategic objectives and that it is done in the most efficient way. Systems deal with the question "Why" (the purpose of the work); "What" (the specific objectives of the work); and "How" (the process used to do the work). Failing to have a predefined system in place will have your agency caregivers and administration staff doing things in random ways with poor efficiencies. You cannot expect that your staff are going to come up with efficient systems – or ways of doing things.

I will never forget the time I had to talk with a staff member about her lack of completing some projects that had been assigned to her. She became defensive and immediately began to tell me how she was spending hours each day opening up some documents one at a time that she would then print and file away. Immediately, I realized that we were lacking a system of operations concerning the files she was wasting precious (expensive) hours of production on. A simple change to electronic upload turned a task that was wasting 3 hours a day into a task that could be performed in under 30 minutes, freeing her up to do more meaningful work.

Each of your business operations should be designed around systems and then your people should run the systems. Without systems, the business will run the people.

CHAPTER 3

The Master of Everything is a Master of Nothing

For more than 20 years, I have been an entrepreneur. During that time, I have sold tacos, ran care homes, started a vocational training school, done home health, built brand new care homes, sold cooking classes, did caterings, ran a $2 Million dollar full-service restaurant, gone back to school, took the MCAT, opened a bar, and managed to raise 5 babies. While I love to stay busy and welcome new challenges, I will be the first to tell you that I often felt overwhelmed throughout the years. I'm talking felt like I was literally drowning trying to keep up. Through a basic lack of wisdom, one of my biggest faults was being unable to say NO. So I kept going, day after day, trying to do it all.

When I look back over this time, I can honestly say that while it all helped get me to where I am today, I would definitely tell my younger self that she must understand this philosophy – The man who tries to be the master of everything will end up being a master of nothing! I lived it! You might look at the list above and say, "Wow! You are a Wonder Woman," but I could tell you that while I did manage to do all of the above, so many of the things on that list only operated at about a 50-60% of what they could have.

It is nearly impossible to do everything and everything at the same time and master it. I often hear new agency owners that have only been in business for a short time say that they are going to start a staffing agency, medical transportation, a group home, or a CNA school. While I would never discourage someone for reaching for the stars and challenging themselves to new heights, if I were to ask them details about their current agency, it would be obvious the untapped markets that they have yet to capture. I challenge you – before adding a single other thing to your plate or list of businesses, ask yourself if you are running efficiently and at your maximum profitability. Because if there is even one hole in the foundation, you should not start another adventure until you have fixed your boat.

You see, by trying to do 10 different things at one time, it was physically impossible for me to be in more than one place at a time. Which meant that I had to assign priority to each business and task that needed to be done. I set up my CNA school back in 2009 and by 2011, it was basically able to run on auto-pilot. However, by 2013, because of my lack of attention, while we remained profitable, I realized that our profit had dropped in half from when I was fully engaged in the business. By 2016, a local competitor who only did one thing – run a school, had stepped in and grew her business to a level where she far surpassed what my school offered – she offered 10 short-term training programs. And not only did she offer 7 more courses than my school, she also began offering hybrid and online courses – doubling her student enrollment. It would take me a whole year to work to build and incorporate an online training component to our school, and another year before we launched our 4th course. Not because I wasn't as smart or ambitious as her – but because she had the time and focus to dedicate to her business, while I was in the middle of trying to save a failing restaurant and bar. Because they were costing me money, I had to put my effort and attention on them, not on developing something that would actually grow our revenue. I lost out on more than 6 years of increased revenue and keeping up with our local market's competition.

Start with one Focus

Decide what will be the primary focus for your agency. Whether serving a specific population such as Brain Injury patients, Dementia, or basic non-medical caregiving- Set your goal and don't stop until you reach it. As you go, ensure that you are establishing Operating Systems so that your team has a guide to follow. Set metrics that can easily be defined and measured. For example, my staffing team know that our agency goal is to staff 92% of all billable hours within our agency. It is easy to see if they have met the goal on a weekly basis. We add up how many hours we had that were billable and how many hours we actually did staff to get the percentage of billable hours staffed. Until you reach your goal, you cannot allow yourself or your team to be distracted with any new ventures. Commit to your primary focus until it is operating at 95% or higher and than consider adding additional services or a new venture. Remember, any new venture or project is only going to pull away from your current goals if they are not already being met.

Empower your Leadership

Do the members on your team have the authority to make major decisions without having to go through you? Another proverb you may have heard that says the same thign is "The Jack of all trades, master of none." If your team is not empowered to be able to act independently of you and must run everything through you, then you could also be guilty of being the jack of all trades, master of none. You must be willing to remove your hands from every single decision and being the final say. You cannot do it all. And you should not want to do it all. Running a successful Homecare agency will require you to surround yourself with people who may even possibly be smarter than you and capable of executing on the things that matter without having to go through you.

Grow Slowly and with Purpose

Avoid FOMO at all costs! Allowing the Fear of Missing Out to guide the decisions you make as an agency owner can cost you in the long run. It is easy to see a Facebook post of someone saying that they are starting their CNA school or transportation company and feel like you should be adding to your business plan or risk being left behind. Human nature makes us compare ourselves to the next person, always looking to have what they have or more than them. Don't get caught up in this game! Only you can evaluate if your agency is doing all that it can right now in this moment. Only you can decide that you are in a stable financial place and have the time and resources to add to your existing services. Entrepreneurship is a long-game. It is not a get rick quick scheme or making poorly researched decisions.

Before you start on your next venture, be sure that you have researched it. Create a business plan and set goals. Think purposefully and ensure it aligns with your values and long-term plans and goals.

Always let your next move be your best move – not a move you make to keep up with someone else!

CHAPTER 4

Your Dream Team

Behind every financially successful person is a Dream Team. Remember in the last chapter where we talked about trying to master everything? Your agency's future financial success will depend on the decisions that you make today, so it is imperative that you surround yourself with people smarter than you.

Your Dream Team should be built of people you turn to for financial, accounting, and legal advice. They are a team of people who look out for your and your best interest. With so many things having been affected by Covid-19, establishing your Dream Team is more essential than ever before. Building your Dream Team will take time and effort but having people on your side will more than justify the cost. Here are some steps to help you find the best fit:

Find an Accountant

With so many changes to the world economic state, a good accountant will be able to keep you up to date and help you to anticipate changes you need to make. Should you be an LLC or an S-Corp, how much should you be paying in estimated taxes – all of these are questions that a good accountant will be able to help advise you on that is best for your particular situation. In addition to finding an accountant through word of mouth, don't hesitate to accept a recommendation from your lawyer or tax preparer. Your Dream Team will have to be able and willing to work together.

Your Certified Public Accountant will be your number cruncher. They should specialize in tasks like preparing and reviewing your financial reports, building income statements, and preparing your tax returns.

Ask the accountant if they belong to any professional organization that includes a set of ethics and requires continuing education. Find out how they feel about tax savings and if they regularly evaluate their clients situation to find tax savings. Find out who will be filling out your return and whether they will be able to represent you in case of an IRS audit. Be sure that you understand how you will be billed and approximately how much their services will cost.

You have many options for how you choose to work with your accountant – you can have an in-house bookkeeper and have your accountant perform a monthly or quarterly audit. You can also have your accountant perform all of your monthly bookkeeping, ensuring that your taxes are paid and your accounts reconciled. At a minimum, you should plan time to meet with your accountant in the Fall to review your financial goals – did your company increase or decrease revenue and what your predictions are for the following year. It is the perfect time of year to decide on any changes that may be necessary for the following year.

No matter what happens, always keep in mind that you are ultimately responsible for everything on your tax return. You must be sure that all information reported is accurate. If you aren't sure or are confused, its up to you to quiz the preparer until you are comfortable with the information on the return. Listen to your gut instincts. A good accountant will take the time to explain what they have done for you and why they are advising you a certain way. If they won't explain, it's time to look elsewhere.

Choosing a Lawyer

The best offense is a good defense. Finding a business lawyer was one the best decisions that I ever made. Within about 6 months of finding our current lawyer, I remember thinking that I'm not sure why I ever thought I could continue in business without her. She is truly worth her weight in gold. My family was a bit spoiled when it came time to find a lawyer – we talked with our financial advisor and he made sure he understood enough about us to make good recommendations. He then offered to set up a speed dating session, where we were able to meet with 4 different lawyers for about 20 minutes to ask questions and get a feel for their style and interaction. Ultimately, we chose a younger lawyer, as we felt that she could grow with us and our businesses.

Your business lawyer should be able to do a variety of things for you – everything from reviewing leases and contracts, filing your LLC annual renewals, offering advice on different employee situations, to helping with tax planning. Be sure and find a lawyer with enough business experience to help you in a variety of ways or that is within a firm where they can go to fellow lawyers for information when needed. You want someone that you are comfortable approaching – ask them how you would be able to communicate with them and listen to the answers that they provide. Do they appear to be engaging and open or do they give you short answers? At the foundation of this relationship you will need to be able to build trust, so it is imperative that you are comfortable communicating with them.

Of high importance is their experience or attitude towards tax savings. As a true American, I have no problem paying my share of what is owed to our government, but I don't want to pay a penny more than I should. A good business lawyer will help you find tax savings and be knowledgeable of all coming tax law changes. I have found that my lawyer is more tax savings aggressive than my accountant. She has regularly communicated with my

CPA advising them of a change that was coming and what my business needed to do to be prepared.

Just like with your accountant, you will want to ask about the lawyers experience, how you will be charged, what the approximate cost will be, and whether the lawyer or an associate will handle your issues. A good attorney will help you to make legally sound financial decisions and represent you in any legal matters that come up.

Certified Financial Planner

A Certified Financial Planner is the person that is going to help you manage your personal and financial wealth. Not sure if you currently have wealth that needs managed? Claim your future wealth now and get prepared. Your CFP will help you to monitor and strategize the use of the money you do have coming in and out of your accounts.

Insurance Agent

Your Dream Team must have a good insurance agent that will help you understand the many risks you and your business could face. They can also be a great resource to use when determining the amount of financial coverage needed and ensure that you have the right kind of coverage. I prefer an insurance broker – someone who shops your insurance needs out to a variety of companies versus an agent that represents a single brand. It is a good idea to always run any new coverages by the other members on your Dream Team – particularly any insurance that provides investments, as they may have better ways for you to invest than through insurance.

Banker

Your banker is who you will go to when you need to set up credit card processing, loans, and checking and savings accounts for both your personal and business life. Never underestimate the value of having a relationship with your banker. Last year when PPP loans were first offered, the only businesses that were able to access the money quickly and easily were those who had established relationships with local bankers. Big banks failed their customers initially. I recommend that you choose a local bank where you can work to build a relationship with someone who knows your name and can understand your unique needs.

Business Coach

Last, but certainly not least, I recommend that you invest in a quality business coach. There is a saying that I love to remind others about, "If you are the smartest person in the room, you are in the wrong room." A business coach will act as your motivator, assessor, guide, and counselor as you go from a start-up to a seasoned business owner. They are not meant to do the work for you. Instead, they should push you in the right direction, offering guidance, encouragement, and accountability to help you and your business reach your full potential.

Can you afford a Dream Team?

I'm here to tell you that you can't afford NOT to have a Dream Team. I often hear new business owners say, "I can't afford it. I will have to have my family help me or just figure it out." This thinking is a big reason that many start-up business owners struggle or fail. I can not even begin to list all the ways that I cost myself time and money, by the lack of having a professional to help me along the way. The school of Hard Knocks is not Free, my friend. Ignorance comes at a cost and you simply don't know what you don't know. If you want to build a business that can compete against the best of the best and is built on a solid foundation for the long haul, you will need to build your Dream Team of professional advisors who know how to make that happen. Finding team member who skills and personalities balance each other will cause your business to achieve 100 times more than those with the wrong team or no team at all.

Your Dream Team should be a team of players who can listen to your ideas, challenge you, correct you, refocus you, direct you, mentor you, balance you and help you. It is crucial that you select members that are top-notch in their own field and who will work together with your best interests in mind.

CHAPTER 5

Inner Circle

Get the Right People on Your Bus and then Make Sure They are in the Right Seats

I read a fantastic book by Jim Collins called, *From Good to Great*, that explained this concept so well. Imagine that your business is a bus. A big, old-fashioned school bus that is headed towards its destination – success and whatever that looks like for you. In order for your business to be successful you must surround yourself with others that complement you and fill in the gaps that you lack. You must fill your bus with the right people and then you must ensure that you have the right people in the right seats. It's not enough to surround yourself with others. Collins wrote, "Those who build great organizations make sure they have the right people on the bus and the right people in key seats before they figure out where to drive the bus. When facing chaos and uncertainty, and you cannot possibly predict what is coming around the corner, your best "strategy" is to have a busload of people who can adapt to and perform brilliantly no matter what comes next."

He goes on to say that we must understand 3 simple truths.
1. Beginning with "who" rather than "what," will allow you to more easily adapt to a changing world. If people join the bus because of where

it is going, what happens when you get 10 miles down the road and need to change direction? You will have a big problem on your hands. But if people are on the bus because of who else is on the bus, then its much easier to change direction. "I got on this bus because of who else was on this bus, if we need to change direction, fine with me."

2. If you have the right people on the bus, the problem of how to motivate and manage people largely goes away. The right people don't need to be tightly managed or fired up: they will be self-motivated to by their inner drive to produce the best results and to be part of something great.

3. If you have the wrong people, it doesn't matter whether you do discover the right direction, you still won't have a great company.[1]

If your agency is a bus and you must fill the seats with the right people, what are you looking for?

Staffer

Why is the Staffer listed first, you might ask? Because at the very center of your agency is the one thing that you must do absolutely well in order to be successful – staff your clients. You will have no need for a biller, a nurse, someone in HR, an accountant or attorney if your agency fails to get this one right. Without successfully staffing your clients, whether Medicaid or private pay, you will not have an agency. What good is it to have clients if you are unable to successfully recruit and retain caregivers to staff them? You won't be able to keep any clients you might have and there will be no need for new clients if you do not have someone in this role that is a great fit. Notice I did not say a good fit, but a great fit.

---

1 Jim Collins, *From Good to Great*

The most essential role in your office, your staffer must be someone with excellent communication and organizational skills, have the ability to adapt and be extremely flexible, and have an amazing aptitude for resilience – able to let any and everything roll right off their back and bounce right back. This role will never work with someone who is incapable of being flexible and as I love to say – unable to live in a world of gray. Staffing and dealing with people is rarely a black and white world. You have to be able to look for the good, and be okay with what you get, knowing that some of the greatest caregivers will be flawed.

I remember one point where I was in desperate need of a new staffer to add to our team. I searched high and low, looking for someone with experience to fill my position. I kept telling my team to be patient, I knew that they needed help and was trying to find what felt like a unicorn. Until one day, I had an a-ha moment and thought that I should instead try to find something that I saw everyday. I went down the list of people that I knew/had worked with before and narrowed down my list to people who I knew were excellent caregivers themselves and even included some moms on my list who had a lot of children. It was then that I discovered that if I found someone with some of the traits that I needed – I could train them into what I needed them to be. I was able to take a caregiver and a mom of 5, who already had the skills of good communication and organization as well as definitely knew how to be flexible and multi-task, and then teach them how to take that experience and be able to staff. And let me tell you now – It has been the best decision ever! Don't wait to find the perfect staffer – identify the skills that are the most important to you in a person and teach the rest!

Key Points to remember for your staffers
How much is too much for a staffer and how will you know when you need to add to your team? We have found the sweet spot for one staffer is not based on the number of clients, but instead on the number of hours they are responsible for staffing. Our target per staffer is around 2,500

hours and as much as 3,000 hours if you include your night hours staffed. Usually when we are near the 2,000 hour mark for a staffer, we begin our search for a new staffer.

Pay and Bonus Plan. I believe that any role that is directly tied to metrics that drive your agency should be rewarded with an incentive based plan. You want your staffer to know that if they hit the established goals they will be rewarded for their effort. We therefore offer competitive hourly pay and then a bonus plan. You will want to set your agency's goals – for our agency in this pandemic, our target goal for our staffers is 92% of all billable hours. Then you can break their bonus down into parts – hours billable each week, hours of overtime, and even exceeding the established goals. Our bonus plan for staffers is set to pay up to 25% of their annual salary on a monthly basis.

Biller. Next to your staffer, another important role is that of your biller or bookkeeper. Understand that they don't have to be the same person. In our agency, with a high percentage of Medicaid clients, our billing is a full-time job by itself. While your staffer must embody the very definition of flexibility, your biller will be the exact opposite and should rigidly follow structure and consistency. Whoever fills this role within your agency, they must have the following characteristics:
- Be conscientious and detail oriented
- They must be methodical – slower is definitely better
- They must be a critical thinker – it's never as easy as clicking a button. They must be able to take information from one puzzle piece and make it fit in another situation. They must be able to deduce answers from pieces of information that they are given
- They must be inquisitive – You need a person that is going to ask questions. If a payment is denied, you need someone who knows that they need to investigate and figure out what went wrong. They can't take things at surface value. They truly must understand why they are doing what they are doing.

I remember someone that I hired for this role because she had ran her own business and had experience with quickbooks and "billing." Well, let me tell you – generically billing invoices to clients is not the same as billing insurance companies. It took me about 9 months, or 3 months too long to realize that although she was a stellar employee, highly organized, efficient, and motivated, she did not have the level of attention to detail that my billing required and ultimately cost me more than $25,000 in billing errors or omissions. A perfect example of having the right someone on my bus, but in the wrong seat!

As your agency grows and your payroll costs increase, you will understand the critical need for precision and detail in order to ensure that your revenue is regularly coming in. Take your time with this hire. Again, I have successfully trained several people into this role that did not necessarily have "medical billing experience." Instead, I made sure that they had the necessary skill traits above and was able to build on that knowledge. My advice to you – I would not hire anyone for this position without having them complete a personality test. There are plenty out there for you to use, but I prefer the DISC method. Research different ones and be sure that you understand the different personality types of the one you choose. For the DISC method, your biller should be a strong C type.

Payroll and Bookkeeping

Similar to the traits of your biller, whoever does your payroll and bookkeeping must be someone you can trust and who pays attention to detail. As your agency grows, your exposure to being exploited and stolen from increases as well. I remember hiring a lady to do my payroll that had been working for another Home Care agency for at least 5 years. I thought I had hit the jackpot because I found someone with true experience that would be able to walk right in and get started. She worked exactly 5 days for me and during that time did a great job. Asked all the right questions, correctly calculated, and ran her first payroll. On that first Friday, I had an all-day orientation scheduled that started every hour on the hour with our staff for our annual insurance enrollment. Of course, there are always caregivers who complain that their pay was incorrect or they forgot to submit a timesheet and we usually will have to make 2-3 corrected paychecks on a Friday. She brought me the first one to sign and then I assumed she had taken the others to my sister for signatures. The following morning, as I was reconciling my payroll account, I remember coming across a check for almost $700 that was not on my list. I opened the check image and my heart almost fell into my lap – it was a check made out to her. Immediately, I wondered if for some reason I had not explained our payperiods – but I knew that she wouldn't have expected to be paid the very first week she worked – literally on the 5th day. I tried to call and text her and got no answer. I flew up to my office to look in the payroll computer to see what else I could see and guess what I found – Not only had she created a check for herself that she used my stamp to sign, she had also DELETED the check from our payroll program. It did not exist at all!

That experience opened my eyes to start identifying all the ways that someone could steal from me. Had she only been patient and bid her time, she could have took me to the cleaners! She could have made smaller checks that blended in better – our average check was between $3-400 weekly, and used other peoples names – her sister, brother, cousin, or uncle. I would have never known the difference. We were at a point of growth with about 150 employees that I no longer knew every employee's names. Whoever you hire to do your payroll and bookkeeping - you must be able to trust. Is the moral of the story that you need to do your own payroll? Absolutely not! Your valuable time is wiser spent elsewhere. But, there are some simple things you can to do to limit your exposure to theft:

- **Keep any signature stamps locked up.** If I am out of the office and they need to create a check that I cannot sign in person, I have my stamp locked up with another key staff member. This way the payroll person has to take it to them and I have a 2-person verification for the use of the stamp.

- **Never allow the person doing your books to be able to write or cash checks** – Another incredible safeguard, you will want to create two-step processes and then divide the steps between two different people. Whoever does your bookkeeping, should not do your payroll or have access to creating checks! If they are creating the numbers and controlling the entries in your records, they control what you see. You need these to remain two separate and distinct roles – Your bookkeepers ethics must remain impeachable and protected – she is the first watchguard for any discrepancies of your payroll. As a start-up that might mean that your bookkeeper does all of your entries and billing, but you pay the bills, write the checks and make deposits.

- **Learn to recognize behaviors** – Some signs to be watchful for are living beyond their means, addiction, having financial difficulties, having close relationships with vendors, having control issues. and drastic life changes like divorce, discontent and revenge. Any of these signs can signal someone with the potential to steal from your company. Never say what someone won't do!

- **Review your payroll** – Within our agency, we follow a procedure of having our payroll staff complete all calculations and entries and then one of us owners approves the file before it is sent off and signs any checks.

- **Don't allow someone in payroll or bookkeeping to take work home** – this does not preclude you using a contract vendor for these services that are performed off-site.

- **Always ensure that your accounts are reconciled monthly.** Hire an outside source like your CPA to review and reconcile your accounts on a monthly or quarterly basis at a minimum. Our ageny's bookkeeper does all of the daily and weekly entries and maintains the books, while I have our CPA reconcile and look for any irregularities.

- **Communicate your message about employee honesty** – From the first date of hire and regularly thereafter, remind your employees of the expectation for honesty and transparency in all their actions.

Your best choice for a Bookkeeper and Payroll staff is to ensure they are able to avoid mistakes and have a great attention for details– I'll never forget the time that I sent a weekly employee a direct deposit for more than $2,000, simply because I entered too many hours and wasn't paying attention. She happened to be honest enough to immediately tell me what had happened, but I know of plenty other caregivers who would have just quit rather than return the money.

Marketing

One of the first faces that your potential customers or referral sources will meet, your marketer should have excellent spoken and written communication skills, a create and open-minded approach, strong organizational and planning abilities, and proven leadership qualities. A good marketer will drive processes and be able to motivate others to see the end goal while completing day to day tasks. They must be able to work under pressure and meet deadlines. In order for your agency to market successfully, your marketer must be able to communicate your message effectively – it is important that you find someone who has the ability to engage your audience from the start. They have to be able to convey what sets your Home Care agency apart from the competition. They must:

- **Be Curious** – A successful marketer must be able to observe who they are speaking to in order to understand their motivations and what will make them fall in love with your agency. They need a curious mind that is always asking questions to better understand a customer in order to explain how your agency will meet their needs.

- **Be a Salesman** – A good marketer is great at selling. They should be able to sell ice to an eskimo. They have to know how to approach your potential customer and sell them on why your agency is the right choice.

- **Be Innovative** – They can't be afraid to try out new ideas and strategies. Just because something has worked before, does not mean that it will always work. They have to be willing to do research and be open to trying alternative methods.

- **Be Adaptable** – They must be willing to evolve with the changing world and ready to react and adapt to new trends.

- **Be Creative** – In order to be successful, your chosen marketer has to know how to distinguish your Homecare agency from the crowd. They have to know how to make your service attractive, helping your potential customer or referral source to see things from a different angle, making you stand out.

- **Be a Relationship Builder** – Another trait of a successful marketer, they must be able to build rapport and relationships with those around them. They must be able to build a strong network of relationships. It is crucial that they are able to get along well with both co-workers and clients.

- **Be a Good Observer** – Since marketing is all about identifying and satisfying your client's needs, being good at observing others is a key trait of a successful marketer. They must be able to identify their target audience, their needs, and offer a solution on how to satisfy them.

The success of your Homecare agency will depend on how well you sell your agency and your services to those in need. It is vital that you have someone in your inner circle who embodies the traits above, because if they lack in any one area, the results will tell.

You must take great care when selecting the members of your inner circle. Not everyone will work well in a team environment. Your team's success at teamwork will depend on them being able to cooperate, be flexible, and be able to collaborate amongst each other. As the agency owner, you must promote an environment that nurtures confidence, participation, and contribution. Your team members must be willing to listen and to adapt. They must share a commitment to:

- Team success and shared goals
- Interdependence combined with an understanding that more is achieved together than separately.

The team and what is best for your business must take preference over personal goals and egos. Successful teams are motivated and engaged. They strive for the business success rather than their own.

CHAPTER 6

Leadership

Help enough people to get what they want and you will have
everything in life that you want.
—Zig Ziglar

Did it escape your attention that I did not include an Administrator role in the previous chapter of who to have in your inner circle? As your agency grows, the time may come where you can afford and need to hire someone to fill this role. But as a startup, and indeed in your early years, that role will most likely fall to you. Your Dream Team and your Inner Circle will be looking to you to lead and guide your agency.

Your goal as a Homecare agency owner is to be successful, to help others, and to fulfill your potential as a person in everything that you do. The key to your great success story is going to come through the principle of "leverage." It is locked in your ability to leverage your talents and skills like a multiplication sign through other people that enables you to accomplish extraordinary things in a short amount of time. **There is no place where leverage is more important than your ability to influence others in such as way that they help you to get things you want while at the same time they are helping themselves to get the things that they want.**

One of the laws of life is something called the "Law of Reciprocity." This law says that people will always try to pay you back for anything that you do – good or bad, either to them or for them. In a good way, it means that if you do something nice for another person, you create within that person a sense of obligation. Since no one likes to be under obligation to another person, the other person will do whatever they can to free themselves from that obligation by paying you back, and oftentimes giving you back more than you originally gave them.

Over the last 21 years of raising my 5 children, I can't tell you how many times I have had to call to make a last-minute order for a birthday cake from a local bakery. More times than I care to admit, I have had some outstanding people jump in to cover for my lack of planning, providing me with an exceptional cake and rave reviews. What do you think that I did in return for the service they provided me – every time anyone talked about cake, I in-turn would give a recommendation of exactly where they should go to get their next cake. It didn't matter whether it was on Facebook or in-person, I sang their praises to anyone who even thought about mentioning cake. While I can never know exactly the amount of revenue I sent to that little cake shop, I do know that it far exceeded the $50 purchase that I made. This is what is amazing about the Law of Reciprocity – the repayment you receive for doing something nice for someone can far outweigh your original contribution.

A defining success principle for a good leader is this, "The more you give of yourself without expectation for return, the more you will get back from the most unexpected sources." How many times have you seen a Homecare agency owner make an inspirational post on Facebook to say that follow-ing an interaction, a caregiving relationship, or a care planning meeting, that they received calls and offers of more business? Or have you, yourself received a referral from a client with minimal hours that resulted in gaining a client with 24-hour care? This success principle of sowing and reaping, combined with the Law of Reciprocity, if taken to heart, will distinguish you as a leader that will make others want to follow you.

The most successful leaders in our society are always looking for opportunities to contribute to others, knowing that they are sowing the seeds that they will reap in the form of power, influence, and desire in others to cooperate and assist them at a later time.

Dwight D. Eisenhower once said, *"Leadership is the ability to get people to do the tasks that you want to them to do and think of it as their own idea."* In order to create a successful Homecare agency, you will have to learn the art of leverage. You will have to be able to take your talents and abilities and multiply them times the talents and abilities of many other people. Referred to as "OPE," or Other People's Effort, your ability to attract people who will willingly work hard to help you to be more successful while they are helping themselves is critical. In order to grow and sustain a thriving Homecare agency, you must learn how to tap into the energy and efforts of lots of people at all levels.

A sense of ownership

One way to leverage your team's efforts is to convey a sense of ownership into the tasks that they will perform. When a person "owns" a task, they have an innate responsibility for seeing that it is not only done but done well. When you clean in your own home, you don't half-way do the job, do you? You do it right because it is your home and something that you are proud of. Have you ever told your teen to clean a bathroom and came behind them only to find that they did a piss-poor job, leaving tasks half-done? They did the job you asked them to because they had to, but not because they accepted ownership of the task and cared about the final outcome. It was done simply because they were required to do it. In order for your inner circle to perform well and for your agency to grow, you will need to develop the ability to transfer ownership into the mind and hearts of your team. So, how do you do this?

To transfer ownership of a task to someone else, you will first want to have a pre-defined goal in mind – what the end result of the task should be. Bring it up to your team casually, but thoroughly discuss the subject, asking for their ideas and input, as well as suggestions on how to best do the job. Allow time for actual thought and conversation – don't allow a sense of hurry to creep in or you will risk the conversation turning into a command that they are not invested in. After a thorough discussion, covering all the critical needs of the task, give your team both the authority and encouragement to do the job within a certain time and to a certain standard. Set a fixed date for you to both meet again allowing them the opportunity to report back on the outcome and results.

I will never forget the time I told my team about an upcoming awareness month, about 3 months in advance. I sent the three of them an email and told them that it was coming up and I expected them to do something big to celebrate and acknowledge this particular month. I didn't follow up or have any discussion with them about ideas or input, but simply expected that they would do what they had been told to do. About two days before the month began, I called the three of them together and asked them to tell me what they would be doing in response to the email that I had sent. I was met with blank stares and one person stammering to say that they had a few ideas of some t-shirts to order. Did you forget that I told you I "told" them what to do 3 months previously? Just like with the teen that you told to clean the bathroom, they had no vested interest in carrying out my command and hadn't given it much thought. The end result was a last-minute thrown together celebration and a very upset leader. I was so angry that they had failed to follow my command that I had specifically told them to do with plenty of notice, that I had to get up and leave the room so that I didn't say anything in anger. It wasn't until later when I had calmed down and replayed the situation in my mind, that I realized my mistake. I failed to use strategy. To get the results that I wanted, which was a creative undertaking that would have been on top of their ordinary daily duties, I should have conveyed ownership of that task. You see, if my approach would have been to meet and brainstorm with my team, allowing them the chance to explore ideas together that they could get excited about bringing to life (because the ideas were theirs), I would have had a completely different outcome. It would not have mattered that it was extra work for them to do on top of what they already were expected to do each day. Their innate sense of accomplishment and achievement would have kicked in and they would have given the task their very best.

Using leverage to Earn your Influence

In order to leverage yourself and grow your agency, you will need other's people's intelligence and other people's cooperation. You need to be able to attract into your life and cultivate the help, assistance, influence and active involvement of lots of other people in achieving your goals. In order to earn the support and assistance of other people you must always look for ways to help them get the things they want so they will be predisposed to helping you to get the things that you want. You really can accomplish anything you want in life by simply finding ways to help other people to accomplish the things that they want. For example, you can grow your agency's revenue by caring for more clients, If you provide consistent, competent caregivers that an Assisted living facility could count on. Somewhere in your local area is a case manager or social worker who needs to find a company that she can refer clients to and count on services being provided consistently and competently so that her job is a little easier. Help her and you end up helping yourself!

All of your relationships are a function of time. In order to be successful as a leader of your team and inner circle, you must invest time in your human relationships, asking questions and listening attentively to the answers. You must make a habit of listening far more than you talk. And the more the other person feels free to talk and express themselves, the more open they will be to being positively influenced by you. The more a person feels like you care about them, and this feeling will happen as a natural extension of you spending time listening to them, the more open they will be to being influenced by you. Taking time to ask people about their lives, to actually listen to their answers, and finding ways to help and support them outside of your business relationship, all show that you care. These acts will help to build a relationship built on respect.

Your ability to influence others on your team and in your inner circle as a leader to help you and cooperate with you, to give you their efforts, their ideas, and their support is the key to you accomplishing extraordinary things in your life and growing your agency into a success. The more people that you can attract into your life that will help you and work with you, the more successful you will be and the faster you will accomplish your goals.

Leadership – Giving without an expectation

In order to become a great leader, you must give up the concept of ME and instead focus on WE. There is a shared underlying need for all humans – we all want a sense of purpose. We want health and well-being. We want happiness and fulfillment. We want meaningful relationships and we want to be financially comfortable. When we see ourselves helping others, we achieve all of these things. If you choose to focus on money first, you will inevitably miss one or more of the other things.

It is impossible to grow your agency without learning the art of leverage – multiplying your ideas and needs through a team of people in your inner circle, using their efforts, energy, ideas, and imagination. In order to gain a team that is willing to be positively influenced by you as their leader, you must develop the skill of being a leader that focuses on developing relationships and putting the needs of others first. By doing so, you will get everything that you, yourself need.

CHAPTER 7

Your Vision

Then the Lord answered me and said, "Write the vision and make it plain on tablets, that he may run who reads it. For the vision is yet for an appointed time. But at the end, it will speak, and it will not lie. Though it tarries, wait for it; Because it will surely come, It will not tarry."
—Habakkuk 2:2-3

Without a vision and a plan, it will be impossible for your agency to succeed. Without a clearly defined map of what you are working towards, it will be easy for the trials and traps of entrepreneurship to creep up and drown out your focus. So, what is a vision? A vision is a practical guide for creating plans, setting goals and objectives, making decisions, and coordinating and evaluating your efforts. Your agency's vision is what will keep your agency focused and together, especially in the stressful days of your agency's first few years. Having a vision means that you have a clear sense of purpose.

Your vision should be a mental picture of the result you want to achieve with your agency – whether that be to have 50 clients, or make $2 Million dollars, the picture should be so clear and strong it will help to make the result clear. A vision is not a vague wish, or hope, or dream. It should come from the future and inform and energize the present. It is your opportunity to communicate your values and goals.

So why is a vision so powerful and necessary?

A vision inspires action. A clear and powerful vision will pull in ideas, people, and other resources to bring it to life. It will create the motivation to make change happen. It will inspire your team to commit, to persist, and to give their best.

3 reasons you must have vision:

1. **A vision is unifying** – A clear vision provides a common interest that makes everyone feel they are part of a greater whole. It will help to unify everyone into a team that is organized, focused, and working together to contribute to the vision.

2. **It is Inspiring** – A clearly defined vision has a motivational effect on everyone within your agency. It creates an energy and enthusiasm that helps to increase commitment and foster change. Especially important for the healthcare field where you can face countless stressful situations, having a clear vision will produce persistence and remind you why you started the agency in the first place.

3. **It provides a focus for goal-setting and business planning** – Having a vision provides a sense of purpose and direction for your business that allows you to set short and long-term goals and it helps to guide any other decisions you need to make along the way. It provides a measuring stick for all decisions – will this decision steer me closer or farther from our vision?

Define your Agency's Vision

Now that you know why you need a clearly defined vision, here are some important keys to remember when defining yours:

Your vision should:

- **Be Clear** – It should be so sharp and detailed that you can imagine the smallest details. It should clearly clarify purpose and direction.

- **Be Positive** – Acknowledge the difficulties, but don't build your vision on fear of what will happen if you don't succeed. John Graham says that visions built on fear can limit your results, causing you to focus on damage control rather than creating positive change.

- **Be Big Enough** – A vision that is too small might not provide enough inspiration or generate enough energy and could limit your achievements. Your vision should set a standard of excellence and performance and force your team to stretch to reach it.

A Vision Statement

Once you have a clear vision in mind for your company, you need to form a vision statement that you will be able to share with your clients and employees. Each member of your team, regardless of their function within the team needs to know where they are headed so that every action and decision they make will lead to one goal. Your Vision statement will serve two functions:

1. It will develop loyalty in your employees

2. It will maintain loyalty in your clients

When a company is able to create a connection with its employees and clients, it can earn their loyalty for life. You see, your inner circle and caregivers will remain loyal to a company where their needs are met and the potential for future progress is clear. When developing your vision statement, you must know what the vision is, the strategies you will use to get there, and have the discipline to get it done. When writing your vision statement remember it should be:

- **Short** – Only one or two sentences in length, the more succinct your statement is, the more memorable it will be
- **Simple** – Be sure and use simple words that everyone can understand.
- **Provide Strategic Direction** – Paint a picture of where the company is headed.

As the leader of your agency, no one can set the tone for your agency's growth and goals but you and without a clearly defined vision of where you are headed, it will be impossible to effectively leverage your team's abilities and contributions. Don't skip this part and fail to give it the time and th it deserves. It can be the difference in your agency wandering aimlessly from one idea to the next in an attempt to survive or your agency developing a laser focus and achieving great success.

CHAPTER 8

Your Ethics

I would be remiss if I didn't offer you the opportunity to do a check-up on yourself and your habits, actions, and thoughts.

Having a strong foundation of ethical leadership is an essential component of a thriving, reputable agency. There is a big difference in being a boss and being a leader. Where a boss orders, a leader guides; where a boss manages, a leader inspires. The difference is in how you make your employees feel and how you view your relationship with them. A good leader will see it as their responsibility to inspire, guide and nurture their employees to help them improve – they lead by example.

Heather R. Younger, founder and CEO of Employee Fantatix, put it, "an ethical leader is someone who lives and dies for integrity. Doing the right thing, even when it hurts, is the ethical leader's mantra." In order to be an ethical leader, you must understand that your actions, behaviors, and words will be put under a microscope – both in and out of the office. You must demonstrate good values through both your words and actions. According to the Harvard Business Review, ethical leaders will not overlook wrongdoing, even in cases when doing so may benefit their business. Showing integrity and doing what's right are essential traits of an ethical leader.

Many of you are in business as a Homecare agency with the goal of creating financial freedom for you and your family. After gaining just a few clients, you may find that you have a cash flow of more than you have ever experienced at one time. Suddenly having money where you have not had large sums of money before can test even the strongest ethics, especially when you have access to request more through insurance programs. How often have you heard of a medical provider or agency charged with fraudulently billing for services that were not provided? While you may say to me that you would never commit such a crime, I challenge you to do a check-up from the neck up on other ways you could be sabatoging your ethics and sliding down a slippery slope to the very fraud mentioned above.

In my second book, From Plans to Profits, I touched on the issue of whether a caregiver can be a contract worker versus an employee. Often, I have seen people comment in threads that they are going to pay their workers as contractors for as long as they can, despite people offering good advice questioning the legality of this action. They claim to do so for a variety of reasons. But whether on their part or that of the caregivers, the underlying goal is to avoid paying taxes and over-time. While I also don't want to pay a penny more in taxes than I have to, failing to do so places your ethics in question. If you will cheat to avoid paying taxes, what else will you cheat on? I cannot tell you how many caregivers have asked us to "pay them under the table" – pay them in cash so they didn't have to report the income or pay taxes on it. And while it would have saved me money as well, it crosses an ethical line that can jeopardize not only your agency's future, but your reputation as well.

What does your life say about you? If someone seen you on the street or out at the club on the weekend, would they ever guess that you run a Homecare Agency, responsible for the care and well-being of the elderly? When you walk into the bank or a store and are treated funny, what is your response? You must be aware at all times that someone is always watching. What you do, even in your private life, will reflect in your business world and could reflect on your agency's reputation. Before I even consider hiring offering an interview for a position within my company, I start my hunt searching through a person's social media files. If I see that you are cussing, talking crazy or into some sketchy activities or associations, it's a pass for me. I have seen people talking and cussing about their own children – do you think that they will be different behind closed doors with my clients?

Your ethics, beliefs, and attitudes will carry-forward into every area of your business. Regularly challenge your own thinking and choices to be sure that your actions and words are without reproach. Your word and the ability to be able to trust you are one of the pillars to the success of your agency.

CHAPTER 9

Continuous Development

When is the last time that you read or listened to a book about any aspect of your business? When is the last time that you read or listened to any kind of book? What are you actively doing to ensure that you continue to grow and develop as a leader and as a business owner? I am amazed at the number of people who believe that once they walk away from school and have earned their degree that they are done and have no need to pick up a book again.

I challenge you to think about it – when your day is done and you finally have down time, how do you spend your time? Do you flop into bed after a long day to mindlessly scroll through Facebook for several hours or do you settle down to watch your shows on Netflix? Just how do you spend your time?

Lifelong learning is essential for personal and professional growth. It is necessary for you to continue forward progress. Continuous learning is your self-motivated persistence in acquiring new knowledge in order to expand your skillset and develop future opportunities. It allows you to reach your full potential. The wealth of Knowledge that exists today and continues to be formed tomorrow is at your fingertips. It is up to you to be on purpose in your pursuit of it.

5 Key reasons you should be on-purpose in your pursuit of continuous development:

1. Stay Competitive

I will never forget in 2016 when I realized that my CNA training school had been left behind the competition in my area. A no-name school that opened 3 years after we did have crept in under my nose and was stealing a significant portion of my business. How did they do it? They had searched and found a program that allowed them to add a Hybrid option to their courses – allowing students to complete half the program on-line, also doubling the number of courses they could offer with the same number of teachers. We didn't have a single class that was offered online and were losing students who wanted a more modern time option. You have to stay abreast of industry changes within your community and area in order to remain up-to-date so that your agency is not left behind. You must network with decision makers and follow any applicable publications necessary to ensure that you know what is relevant within the Homecare world.

2. Build Confidence

As a new agency owner, there is nothing worse than feeling like you don't know what is going on, or having a potential client reach out to you and explain a situation that you have never heard of before. By actively working to build your knowledge base and continuously learning, you will actually build your confidence and find that it is easier to take on new situations and challenges. Join your area's local Home Care community support groups, contact your state's policymakers, and join your local chamber of commerce. By staying abreast of the latest information and changes within healthcare, you will be able to confidently advocate for your clients.

3. Spark New Ideas

Learning new skills and information will open your eyes to new opportunities and spark ideas for change. I would have never thought about opening a Mental Health Association if I had not developed a relationship with a therapist leading to interesting conversations that sparked the idea of whether this was a service that I could offer. That one idea led me to do research that lead to answers that eventually led to me starting a business called Sound Mind Mental Health Association. In our first year with only 3 therapists, we made $400,000 in revenue and pulled a 50%+ profit margin! All it took was one spark and that same business has now grown to over $1 Million in revenue in only 2 years!

4. Organizational Benefits

Creating and promoting a learning culture within your agency is the most effective way to improve performance and innovation and helps to increase your employee satisfaction and retention. The more your employees and teammates know, the more they can contribute to your organization. I had to learn the hard way that just because someone is good at their job and has natural leadership tendencies does not make them a good leader. A good boss, yes, but good leader – No. Leadership is something that has to be developed and long ago, I learned to require continuous learning from my team leaders. I regularly assign books for them to read or listen to and then we come together to discuss them. I had to learn the hard way that the wisdom to pursue continuous development is not natural in people and that I could not be the only person within my company learning.

5. Upgrade Your Own Skills

Your team is only as good as your leadership. When you upgrade your skills and knowledge set, you are able to pass it on to your team, thereby furthering your business growth. Actively learning and working on skills like interpersonal skills, negotiating skills, and adaptability not only help you to become a well-rounded leader, but will rub off on your team as you influence them.

How can you practice Continuous Learning?

1. Read or Listen to Books

At all times, I carry 1-2 books and have at least 3 downloaded on my phone through Audible. You might try to tell me that you are just too busy, but I challenge you to find the time. Even 15-20 minutes while you are driving from place to place on your marketing day is enough to have listened to a couple of chapters of a book. There is not a waiting room that I sit in that I don't pull out one of my books, quickly reading a few pages while I wait. It doesn't matter the topic or size, any and everything that you pour into your mind will increase its value. I generally like to jot down the name of books that I hear people talk about that have helped them and at any given time can be reading or listening to a variety of topics, from leadership and business management to finances and investment. And I won't forget about my love of Historical fiction!

2. Listen to Podcasts

There are an abundance of podcasts available for you to listen to on a variety of platforms. Your phone – whether Apple or Android, offers multiple apps that will allow you to listen to a podcast that covers subjects from current political news to financial reports. There is a lot of content available that will further your continuous learning and leadership development. Great leaders aren't born – they are made!

3. **Network**

Get out and network! Networking allows you the opportunity to get out and meet new people. There are plenty of learning opportunities available just by getting to know someone new. The broader your network, the more you can learn from others. There is always someone that has done something that you haven't or something that you can learn – even from someone at the same point in the journey as you. Maybe they are doing it different, maybe they have tried what you are now attempting and can offer you a different perspective. Always be open to talking and learning from others. You will be surprised at what you can learn.

4. **Attend seminars and conferences**

With the onset of Covid-19, a lot of public gathering conferences were cancelled. While some were able to change to a virtual gathering, there is absolutely nothing better than meeting likeminded people for jam-packed information sessions allowing you to be exposed to a wealth of knowledge. Never forgo the opportunity to come together and learn! And I am not just talking about the Home Care industry. There are some excellent leadership and motivational conferences that can be absolute game-changers for you – both professionally and personally. Every time I have attended a conference – whether professional or religious, I have walked away with gems of knowledge and a-ha! Moments that made the price of admission worth every penny! Even if you walk away with a No. I will never forget in 2018 my husband and I went to a Home Health Agency conference in Las Vegas that was teaching about the changes that were coming to skilled care the following year. Although licensed to be a full skilled agency, we did not have a single skilled patient and were only considering the option of adding this branch to our agency. Thank God we went to the conference! $2,500 later we knew that a skilled agency did not align with our long-term plans of working smarter and not harder as we began to see retirement in our future. That $2,500 investment probably saved me hundreds of thousands of dollars in costs of me not knowing any better and attempting the next sensible step in our journey of Homecare agency ownership. Don't forget to subscribe to Ditchthescrubs.com so you stay notified of the next conference we are hosting near you!

5. Formal Study

Don't forget about the option of formal study. If you haven't completed your college degree, go back to school. One class each semester will eventually add up. Check into local colleges in your area – many offer distance education offerings for the returning adult student and can give you credit for classes you have taken in the fall. While a formal degree is not required to be a successful agency owner, and the school of Life can teach you plenty, never discount the education you can gain through formal study. You don't have to learn everything the hard way! I wish I could go back to my first years as an entrepreneur and have taken some basic management, marketing, and finance classes. There are so many mistakes that could have been avoided with some knowledge in any of these areas. If you already have your Bachelor's degree – check out some of the master's degrees. Even if your educational background is in the medical field – consider taking some formal business classes to round out your knowledge base and assist you in the operational side of running your agency.

As a busy Homecare Agency owner, you can't afford to NOT be on purpose in your pursuit of continuous learning. One good idea is all you need to make millions. Every change in your life and business comes when your mind collides with a new idea of some kind. Allowing your mind to bump into a new idea will enable you to see things in a different way which can change your future direction. In order to find these new ideas you must place yourself in their path. You should purposefully surround yourself with them.

CHAPTER 10

Systems and Processes

If you have never heard of business operating systems, you are missing an essential piece of creating a successful business and are most likely chained to your business. Without clearly defined systems in place, your business will be unable to run independent of you. In order to prevent becoming a slave to your business you need carefully thought out processes in place that will allow you to stay in control while successfully managing your business.

Just like with a computer, your business needs an operating system in place to organize the way it functions. Your agency's operating system ensures smooth communication between your leadership team and all of your employees. The only way to create a Homecare Agency that run independent of you is to ensure that you have operating systems in place. Two of the best books that I have read about the importance of operating systems is The E Myth by Michael Gerber and Clockwork by Michael Michalwicz. Both changed my way of thinking forever and I highly recommend that you read them as soon as possible.

Essentially, your operating system will be your agency's playbook. In order for you to effectively lead your team, your playbook must layout the expectations for each person on the team. Your agency operating system gets everyone on the same page, with the same vision, and working toward the same goals. Your expectations, processes, and accountability are clearly defined so that everyone is able to work together. If you don't ensure that you have an operating system in place, your agency will face miscommunication, individual and team conflicts, and chaos resulting in long hours, frustration, wasted time and energy, loss of good employees and long-term financial losses.

Further benefits of an operating system include:
- To standardize tasks throughout your agency – No longer will you deal with a caregiver saying that someone else told them to do something different.
- To focus your resources on the central mission and vision of your agency – without a focused sense of direction, your team will be left to do what they think is most important
- To define predetermined activities that your team can expect and plan for – This helps to prevent chaos and burnout from constantly changing the plan time after time
- To drive processes that allow your organization to seek continuous improvement

There are 4 foundational pieces of any business operating system:
1. Define the Target
2. Execute
3. Evaluate
4. Improve

And then Repeat. As you address each area of your operations, from the time a referral or caregiver walks in your door, you will follow the model above and repeat.

So what are the parts of a Business operational system that you should have in place?

1. **Establish your Vision –**
   As mentioned earlier in this book, what mission and vision drive your organization? What is the goal of your agency?

2. **Define your Business Performance Objectives**
   Setting your business goals for the year or quarter establishes targets and can help to drive focus for your agency, helping your team to decide on what is most important. Without specific goals, your team will do what they feel is the most important.

3. **Employee Performance**
   Building a team with high-client satisfaction should be a high priority of your agency. As the agency leader, you can expect to spend time coaching and mentoring your staff – from your office team to your actual caregivers, giving feedback and addressing performance concerns. Make sure that your operating system for evaluating employee performance includes not just a review of their past performance but an evaluation of any additional skills and talents that can be used in your agency. One of your most valuable assets is the ability to promote from within, increasing your agency's employee retention.

4. **Establish your Agency's Communication Standards**
   Your agency needs a communication plan in place that will keep your team informed and that provides a link between your leaders and the other members of the team. I'm not talking about just email and text communication, but a formal plan that will support your business goals. How often do you meet with the members of your inner-team? How often do your staffers communicate with your caregivers? How

often and how are you regularly communicating with your clients and family members?

5. **Conduct a SWOT analysis of your agency**

   A SWOT analysis stands for Strengths, Weaknesses, Opportunities, and Threats and is a wonderful tool that will help you to examine your agency's operations from different angles. Best done with other members of your internal team, you can learn a lot by analyzing different areas of your operations following this standard. By looking at each area and coming up with a list for each category you can pick different areas to focus and take action in that will help your agency to achieve its business goals.

6. **Evaluation and Enforcement of your Business Ethics and Values**

   Just because you believe and act a certain way does not mean that others know that is expected of them while working for your agency. If you don't have a clearly defined policy of acceptable behaviors than your agency's reputation is in danger of being tarnished by the actions of others that represent you. Regularly conduct ethics training for your team and caregivers.

7. **Conduct Client and Employee Satisfaction Surveys**

   You can't possibly know what the issues are if you don't go and find them. Conducting client and employee surveys can give you a clear sense of how things are going and how you are being evaluated. It will help you to identify trends – both good and bad and reveal underlying issues that need to be addressed.

Your agency operations should be designed around systems that are ran by your team. Without operating systems in place, your Business will run you and your team.

CHAPTER 11

The Low Hanging Fruit

My husband, Steven, is an analytical thinker. For as wild and crazy and I can dream and think, he tends to keep me grounded. When I want to run with an idea 100 miles an hour, he is the one in the background thinking through the details. It works! A couple of years ago, he introduced this idea to me and once I was able to fully understand its meaning, it is not something that I have forgotten. If you are reading this book, hopefully, you have already put in the work and have your agency off the ground. Maybe it's not making the profit you desire, but it's up and running and you have some clients. Maybe you're frustrated at your lack of growth and about to make a dangerous mistake thinking it's a solution – so I want you to ask yourself:
1. Does your agency make less than $2 Million per year in revenue?
2. Do you have less than 100 clients?
3. Have you heard of another way to make money and are thinking of adding another business to try to generate more income? Perhaps Non-Medical Transportation, Adult Daycare, or teaching CNA students?

If you answered yes to any of the questions above, I challenge you to wait and think through the following information and be sure that you have picked all the low hanging fruit first.

I want you to think about the current clients that you have right now. Think about the experiences that you have had when you have visited with them. When you went into their homes for their initial home visit, when

63

you performed a safety inspection, when you performed their caregiver's supervisory visits – what did you see? What did they talk about? How else could you benefit them? You see, in front of you right now, you have a group of customers. You have a datebase of customer information – whether past clients or current ones. Before you decide to start another business and then have to worry about finding customers for the new business venture, I want you to ask yourself if you have thought about bringing MORE value to the customers that you already have.

As a successful business owner, one of your goals should always be to think about how you can continue to add more value to the customers you have right now, and we call this the low hanging fruit. It's very easy to fixate and worry about how in the world you will ever get to the apples that are hanging from the very top of the tree and completely miss the apples that are within a fingertips reach still hanging unpicked on the lower branches that are already within reach. Sales professionals will tell you that it is easier to get a current customer to buy additional services or products than it is to find a new customer. Why? Because they are comfortable with you and already know that you provide good service. They don't have to think twice about the next thing that you are offering to them because they trust you.

What problems have you encountered offering services to your Homecare clients? Have you ever thought, I wish that this was different because then we could do our job easier? Is it possible that you can offer that particular service? By offering additional value added services, your Homecare agency will be able to stand out from your competition.

Homecare clients present some unique opportunities for additional income generating value added services that you can offer right now, without having to "start" another business. For example:

- **Weekly or Monthly Home Deep Cleaning** – By simply hiring 1 or 2 housekeepers to add to your team, you could offer a true housekeeping service to the customers that you are already staffing with caregivers

- **Shopping and Supply ordering** - Take the worry off of family members and let them know that your team can perform all necessary shopping and supply ordering for the client and simply add it to the bill – for a fee.

- **Wellness Monitoring** – Have you ever had a client's family member ask you to just "check-in" on their parent? Wellness monitoring allows you to offer a flat fee to do just that – perform a wellness visit, ensuing that their loved one is safe and healthy, while saving them money from paying for your minimum hours of service.

- **Medication Reminder Service** – We found this one so easy to add to our services. There are services that you simply add the client to along with the times for their scheduled calls and it does all the work for you at a tiny cost – like a few pennies per call! You could easily charge $30-50/month for this service.

- **PERS Unit Rental – Personal Emergency Response Services –** Similar to Life Alert buttons these units can be purchased for a small up-front cost and then rented back to the client's for a small monthly price.

- **Respite Care** – Your agency can offer to provide short-term fill-in care.

In addition to adding additional services to your client, don't neglect what's right in front of you. When is the last time you evaluated your client's needs? Have you checked with the caregiver to find out if the client is requiring more care than before? Have their needs changed enough that they require a leveling increase fee or do you need to suggest that need more hours of care? Particularly with Medicaid clients, it is up to you to advocate for the client. Could they benefit from an increase in their current plan of care's authorized hours of care?

Additional Ideas for Revenue:

Once you have picked all of the low hanging fruit by adding additional income generating services to the clients that you already have, now you can start to think about other businesses that you could potentially start. It is always a good idea to stick to services that could benefit one another – each could feed each other business and work together. Some ideas that we have found profitable include:

Non-Emergency Medical Transportation – With a wheelchair accessible van, you can easily begin offering this valuable service. Hospitals and private clients alike are always in need of reliable resources to transport clients to and from appointments and home. You will need to ensure that you have the proper Commercial liability insurances in place – don't dare try to perform this service using personal car insurance as it could be voided in the operation of a business. When your company picks up clients, always have brochures and business cards to leave with potential customers advertising your Homecare agency.

Staffing Agency – Just like you staff clients in their homes, you can offer medical staffing to facilities and other agencies and charge a 50% mark-up on the hourly rate that you pay. You will need to build a dependable pool of qualified staff – most facilities will require that all of your staff are certified or licensed and that your agency is licensed, bonded, and insured, but you have the opportunity to tap into a different class of workers – licensed and registered nurses as well. With hourly pay rates ranging from $25-75/ hour, your profit margins can shoot through the roof once the hourly rate is marked up.

Mental Health – We found that with a lot of our Medicaid clients we were dealing with depression, mental illness, and behaviors and they were in need of a lot of attention when our nurse would perform supervisory visits. It got me to thinking and I researched the therapy benefit for Medicaid clients in Kansas and found out that it was an unlimited benefit – they can literally meet with a therapist – in-person or over the phone, 365 days of the year and Medicaid would pay for it. At the time we had about 200 Medicaid clients and I immediately came up with a new model – we already had the clients, I just needed therapists that we could send to them. 2 years later and we have a fully thriving Mental Health Agency with excellent profit margins.

While you will always want to challenge yourself and reach for the stars in business success, don't fail to see what is right in front of you. Be sure that you have plucked all the fruit that is still hanging low and constantly reevaluate to see if you can find more low hanging fruit.

CHAPTER 12

Pay Yourself First

For about the first 15 years of my entrepreneurial journey, I never took a paycheck. What? You might ask. How on earth did you pay your bills? Well, I did pay my bills, I just used business funds to do so which is a big No-No. Each time I needed to pay a bill or we wanted to take a trip, I would just transfer money from my business account to my personal account and would do what I needed to do. But there was never any money that really "mine." I remember being so frustrated because I would look over at my husband who swiped his card with no regard and bought what he wanted, while I would think that I couldn't buy anything without thinking through whether or not I had the money in the accounts to do so and how much payroll would be that week.

I was literally chained to my bank accounts. Every single day, both at the start of the day and again before the end of the business day which happened to be at 9:45pm CST, I was logging into my bank accounts to see what needed to be moved around where. What needed to be covered and how much payroll still had to come in. When I did the math of how much came in each month and how much was left over, even if we were positive and the report said that there should be $20,000 left over, I looked at my accounts and also had the same question – where is it at? I knew that I had to always have something in the bank to be ready for the next payroll and for years, I rationalized that it must be in there somewhere and that someday when the final payroll was paid, I would still have money come in for a few weeks and that money was all ours.

It didn't matter if we made a $20,000 in revenue or had a month with $250,000 in revenue that came through the account, the end was always the same. I remember a friend telling me about her kids 529 plans and what was I doing to pay for school for my 5 kids and all I could tell her is that as a small business owner, the best I hoped to do was to be able to pay cash for their school when the time came. The thought of "saving" money to sit in an account to pay for school 15 years down the road when I didn't have $10 that managed to stay in my savings account for more than 30 days was as crazy as going to live on the moon in my mind. We WERE profitable many times during these years, but it felt elusive and like something that I could not grasp. Have you ever felt this way? Can you show a track record of not only consistently paying yourself from your business but also saving each month? Remember, as a entrepreneur, you will most likely not have a retirement plan waiting on you, if you are not on purpose with intentional planning and saving now.

Several years ago, I stumbled across a book on Amazon that I believe changed my life in a dramatic way. After 15 years of being chained to my business finances and feeling stuck, I learned of a new way of thinking that changed everything. You have to get your hands on a book called *Profit First*, by Mike Michalowicz. I am going to teach you the four game-changing concepts the book is built on, but I cannot stress to you enough how you have to read and figure out how to apply these concepts to your own finances. It made such a drastic difference in my own life, I know it can in yours as well.

Take your Profit First, and then pay expenses with what is left over – In one sentence, that is the summary of the book and it is a gamechanger. Mike teaches that you should run your business based on what you can afford to do today and not what you hope to make in the future. He says that when

Profit comes First, it is a focus and not forgotten. How often have you felt like you are the very last person to be paid from your business? In Profit First, he teaches:

- Profit is not an event, or something that only happens at the end of a quarter or a year.

- Profit is not something that has to wait until tomorrow. Profit must happen Now and Always. It has to be baked into your business so that it is a constant. Every day, every transaction, every moment. Profit is not an event. It is a habit.

- You cannot grow out of your financial problems and your salvation does not lie in the next high-paying customer. You have to take your profit first and then grow.

- You have to figure out what makes a profit and dump the things that don't.

- When Profit comes First, it is the Focus and not Forgotten

He teaches four simple steps to achieve this mentality:

1. **Every single time you receive a payment, take your profit first and split the balance into several small accounts. With less cash, you will be forced to find innovative ways to achieve more with less. How is that possible?**
   He teaches, "If you get a $1,000 deposit, I am telling you, starting today, transfer $10 into your PROFIT account. If you could run your business off $1,000, you can surely run it off $990. If you get $20,000 in deposits, you transfer $200 into your PROFIT account. If you can run your business off $20,000 you absolutely can run it off $19,800.

You'll never miss that 1 percent. It is a low bar. But something magical will happen. You will start proving the system to yourself. You won't get rich overnight this way, but you will get a wealth of confidence."

2. **Always take Profits First and pay bills last – so you only spend what you can afford.**

I cannot tell you how many times, I have literally said the words that my bills/expenses were out of control and I literally felt like they had taken over. Every single time I paid one thing off, I found another expense had crept up and taken it's place. Following Mike's advice, your bills will be given a budget that they have to fit into and you will be able to start weeding out what is non-essential. Within quickbooks, there is a feature to make EFT payments from your business account to a vendor. I set myself up as a vendor and scheduled weekly auto-payments into my own account. Set it and forget it. Now, three years into following this method, it is absolutely baked into my budget.

3. **Once you have taken your profit, keep it out of sight, out of mind, and hard to access (except for the right reasons).**

When I started following Profit First, I literally took a trip to NY and opened up 2 different checking/savings accounts with banks that did not have a local branch in Kansas. I wanted that money to be as unaccessible as I could make it. Out of sight is out of mind! My deposits were automatically scheduled and it began to grown. Within 3 months, I had a true savings for the first time in almost 15 years of being an entrepreneur and my confidence truly did grow. All of a sudden, I began to think of how I could add to it and as my revenue grew, I increased my profit deposits. It quickly became a lifestyle!

4. **Build a Rhythm.**

Mike teaches for you to (initially) log in daily to check your balances and then manage your payables and allocations twice a month. For some of you, this book may take baby steps. If you are already running your business in the negative, you may have to start out small. Like he says above, if you receive a $1,000 payment, keep $10 for profit. You will never miss the $10 and it won't make or break your situation. The important thing is the habit and being intentional. Each small step will be leading you in the right direction until one day you will look up and have climbed out of the hole and be back in control of your businesses financial health. If you are already profitable, take control of what is yours. Separate your profit from the business and start learning about investing and preparing for your retirement. As I mentioned earlier, as an entrepreneur your future is in your hands. You must be intentional about seeking wisdom and knowledge to ensure that you are prepared for that future and that your needs will be met.

Remember:

Sales - Expense = Profit

CHAPTER 13

Medicaid Secrets for Success

As I have mentioned in all of my books for Homecare, I am a big fan of Medicaid. I know that there are a lot of people out there who say, "I would never take Medicaid. My agency only takes private pay and LTC insurance," and that's okay. I want to share with you some of my own personal experience that has made our pool of Medicaid clients profitable and worth mentioning.

In case you don't know, every state is federally mandated to have a Medicaid insurance program for people who are disabled or low-income. It is your state's black and white card. It is not automatic – people have to request it and qualify through disability or by a lack of assets. There are different options to Medicaid – qualified members can have medical insurance coverage or if they qualify with a functional limitation, they can also add a program called Home and Community Based Services. Under Home and Community Based Services or HCBS, members are divided into different groups called waivers – Here are some of the waivers that you might see in your state:

- **Autism Waiver** – For children/young adults that have been diagnosed with Autism. Can have a very long waiting list

- **IDD – Intellectually Disabled** – Young adults on this waiver are intellectually disabled and in need of support services. On this waiver you might see older teens/adults living with Down Syndrome.

- **SED – Severe Emotional Disturbance** – This waiver supports members with emotional disturbances or psychiatric diagnosis that provide functional limitations in their daily lives. Members on this waiver can commonly live in group settings.

- **Technology Assisted** – This waiver serves infants and children that have a form of technological dependence – whether that be a feeding tube, tracheostomy, or a ventilator, this waiver usually requires that an agency staff the clients with a licensed nurse depending on their care needs.

- **Brain Injury** – Traditional insurance is only required to cover a member's rehabilitation treatment for 6months following an injury, but the BI waiver gives affected members access to continuing therapies and services for up to 5 years following an accident.

- **Physically Disabled** – This waiver is usually one of the largest groups in any state and serves members under the age of 65. We tend to see a lot of adults with mental illness, chronic medical conditions, severe obesity, chemical dependencies, and other conditions on this waiver.

- **Frail Elderly** – Reserved for members over the age of 65, this waiver serves the elderly and acts as a bridge to keep them in the community as long as possible.

Despite the differences in the waivers and who they support, they all share one common goal – to give members CHOICE and to keep them in their home and communities for as long as safely possible.

In order to provide services to any of these members, your Homecare agency must first become an approved provider for your state's medical plans. Over at www.ditchthescrubs.com within our membership portal, you will have access to the links for your state's specific Medicaid office and requirements. Once you have been approved as a provider, I have found the following benefits of Medicaid that make it worth the effort:

1. **You have a guaranteed client base** – Medicaid members can only work with Medicaid approved Homecare agencies. While they are allowed to have a choice, their choice can only come from the list of approved providers.

2. **As the provider, you are in control** – While it is not ideal to be a Homecare agency with a 100% Medicaid pool of clients, you can decide what percentage of your client base you will accept as Medicaid. You can set limits and agree to take 20 Medicaid clients, or 500 hours of Medicaid – the choice is yours.

3. **Medicaid can offer valuable experience to a new agency** – Medicaid and their unlimited pool of members can be a great starting point for a Homecare agency that is struggling to get started. I have seen countless posts on Facebook groups from owners saying they have been in business for six months to a year and have only one client. By accepting Medicaid, they could have still been generating an income and gaining valuable experience of actually getting to run their agency. In my second book, From Plans to Profits, I encourage newly licensed Homecare agencies to begin the process of becoming a Medicaid provider as soon as they are licensed. No one will force you to begin taking Medicaid before you are ready, but to have it as a backup plan if you do struggle to find private pay clients is an invaluable strategy that just might keep you afloat.

- **Guaranteed Income Source** – In over 20 years of being a Medicaid participating provider, I have never had any problems being paid. I can't count how many times over the years that the consistent dollars of Medicaid got us through another payroll, especially if our private pay clients were low. Once you build up your pool of Medicaid, you know exactly what to expect and when to expect it. It has always been the consistent money in the background, while we have seen private pay go up and down in waves.

There are some other unique program considerations for Medicaid that make it attractive to your agency. These include:

- **Each of the waivers has their own reimbursement rates.** They are not necessarily the same for each. You will want to know the rates for each group of members so that you can decide which group to serve. In Kansas, the Frail Elderly waiver pays the most for non-medical care – currently around $16.50/hour of service. (Yes, we are one of the lower paying states.) But, the TA waiver for the ventilator babies pays $40/hour and most local agencies only pay their nurses around $22/hour. Do the research and get to know the rates so that you can make informed decisions.
- **Family members are allowed to work** – My favorite way to pad our agency's bottom line is through the Medicaid waivers that allow family members to provide the care. When a new client comes to our agency that already has their own worker, we essentially become their payroll processor. Our job is fairly simple – onboard the new "employee" and process their weekly payroll. Yes, the reimbursement rate is small - For that PD waiver, we currently only make a profit of $1.45/hour worked. BUT – if I have 500 hours per week of clients that are self-staffed (about 12 clients) my profit is $725 for that week. In order to make that $725 I only had to invest about 2 hours to process their payroll and ensure there were no other issues. Even at my cost of $20/hour for my payroll position, for a $40 investment, I made $685. In a year, that's $35,000 profit and I basically only had to process the same payroll I was going to do anyway! I have had

some Medicaid cases with family members who have been with my agency for more than 15 years! Usually, they can be some of the most dependable income your agency will ever have. You are not depending on them to have enough money for care for 15 years, but you can count on the state to be able to afford their care for 15+ years.

- **Unique opportunities to extend value and earn additional income** – Each of your waivers will have unique services that are included for the members. Some of these offer the opportunity for your agency to not only earn revenue that is in addition to caregiving, but to offer a needed value to your clients. Some examples include:

  › **Wellness Monitoring/Nurse Evaluations** – In Kansas, both of these activities that take less than 30 minutes, pay $42.50 for the visit. This more than pays for our RNs time and are performed upon admission of any Frail Elderly client and then on-going every other month.

  › **PERS Rental** – Remember that personal emergency response system mentioned previously in the book – Medicaid will pay for this service to your agency for every client! This could generate several thousands each month in additional revenue. In Kansas, they pay $40/month for each member.

  › **Respite Care** – Another option for serving Medicaid clients is to simply offer respite care. Short-term periods of continuous care while a family member needs a break. Respite care rates typically mimic private pay rates and require a shorter commitment.

  › **Home-Delivered Meals** – Another potential source of revenue, Medicaid contracts with providers to provide pre-made, reheatable meals to their members. In Kansas, this service pays about $6.50/meal.

  › **Assisted Services** – Clients on Medicaid waivers have a one-time use budget for either equipment/furniture that can assist them or remodeling of their home or bathroom to assist with functional limitations. Because Medicaid does not partner with contractors, they use HHAs to oversee the work that needs done. For example, you would find a contractor to convert a bathtub to a roll-in shower, and Medicaid would pay you to pay both yourself for your service and the contractor for the work. Although I am not handy and wouldn't have a clue what a good price is a for a home remodel or a wheelchair ramp, my husband is very handy and took over this branch of our agency's operations and it created a new revenue stream for our agency.

Despite its bad reputation amongst Homecare agencies, Medicaid presents an opportunity for increased revenue streams and financial padding that your agency can benefit from. I encourage you to take your time to truly learn and understand the different waivers and programs in your state. Look for how you can make the programs work for your agency and your goals.

Made in the USA
Las Vegas, NV
12 November 2023

80682399R00050